The sick love love

F. Guzzardi

The sick love

Printed in the United States of America First Printing 2021 ISBN print 978-1-947488-69-4 Copyrights MediaBook - 2021

Copyrights F. Guzzardi - Hoffmann & Hoffmann Inc. - 2021 Published in USA Printed worldwide

Publisher Hoffmann & Hoffmann Inc.

Imprint MediaBook

Hoffmann & Hoffmann inc. Ponte Vedra Beach, FL 32082

www.hoffmann-hoffmann.org

Welcome
to
MediaBook

"It is inevitable to surrender that we absolutely don't know nothing about us if not vague flashes of memory which are confused, in the illusion of existence, in regret of what we have lost in being born."

F. Guzzardi

Dedicated to the memory of Maria Luisa Siringo

Contents

1

The sick love

We never fall in love by chance

F. Guzzardi

I t is difficult to explain what the suffering of love and more generally love is, but it is easier to say what love is not, that is, when love is sick.

Every sentimental relationship is unique and is also obscure, because it arises from the interior, which is made up of an entire gallery of unconscious ghosts in dialogue with each other. In the unconscious, there are internal images that activate the eros of both protagonists of the couple.

S o, let's start by saying that erotic forces embody a deep desire for selfknowledge, which, however, always occurs in the confrontation with the other, a confrontation full of opportunities but also of gray areas and dangers that push us to love. even where we sense the object of our elusive inaccessible feeling. In this case, some people insist on chasing the other, who embodies a utopia and appears seductive because it represents the strength of a promise, which at least initially makes the victim feel omnipotent, makes him feel grandiose and heroic, that is, capable of eat the whole world, giving the illusion of being able to achieve every aspiration.

Now, however, we must **distinguish healthy love from sick love**; healthy love designates a circular space between me and the other, it is a kind of dance with an unusual rhythm: The rhythm of approaching, of moving away, of presence, of absence, which also is the rhythm of meaning and of the distortion of every meaning, in the face of the unknown that the other person embodies.

The difference between healthy love and sick love is almost invisible, as sick love does violence, it is violent for the psyche. Sick love corrodes self-esteem, diminishes, impoverishes the relationship itself. Because he lives and feeds on the need to want to possess the other, without realizing that this is a paradox, as the narcissistic desire to possess the object of love arises precisely from being possessed by this need.

So it is paradoxical to be possessed by an unconscious complex of this type. Then we cross over into sick love and consequently regress to a childlike style of relationship with the other, that is, we are dependent. When this process is reversible, then we still move in a rather normal environment but when regression escapes the control of the ego and becomes destructuring, it becomes fragmentation of the ego and is no longer a reversible process; therefore we get sick and fall into a deadly addiction.

You see, we in general are moved by the desire to be wanted by others, because we need to live, to be recognized and appreciated. We ask the other to see us as unique, different, more than what we believe we are and in fact, in love relationships the other evokes a new being in us, the other does not offer his attention, in healthy relationships, he does not want to possess us but offer

himself to us and brings out a new being from us. The other releases something new in us attitude to life, so thanks to him, we are better than before and can therefore give more.

The trouble can come after this gift is withdrawn from us and we have not yet made it our own. We have not assimilated those qualities that have emerged in the relationship and in this case we get lost in that room, in the basement of our soul, and the whole story we have lived with that person is turned upside down because we are unable to withdraw our projections and we live in a deadly addiction that impoverishes us. But in reality no love impoverishes, and even if it ends, it was important because it was necessary to bring out

parts of ourselves that we would never contact, so healthy love allows an opening of the narcissistic shell, therefore it is not easy, to some extent, we must allow the other to alter our identity, letting ourselves be led metaphorically elsewhere, that is, into our unconscious. Now, if in our unconscious there are old traumas or humiliating relationships,
letting ourselves be led metaphorically elsewhere, that is, into our unconscious. Now, if in our unconscious there are old traumas or humiliating relationships, abuses, abuses, it is clear that this whole ghost world will be activated and will emerge strongly, arousing fears and resistances.

The narcissistic person who has been traumatized has deep wounds with him that do not lead to a healthy relationship, but he will tend to develop a relationship of power with the victim on duty and this modality will allow him to maintain his defensive barriers. For example, sexual promiscuity is nothing more than an escape from the most intimate and profound relationship that is perceived as too
destabilizing. Here then is that in this case, the regression that the seduced narcissist would experience would no longer be at the service of the ego and therefore has two paths in front of him or he gets sick or abandons the other and runs away.

Typically the narcissist, when he feels that he is getting too involved, feels fear rising and gives up, while the more "bona fide" or rather naive person becomes addicted. The narcissist projects his greed for possession onto the victim, instead of recognizing it within himself, he sees it in the other, projects it into the other, and therefore sees the victim as a sort of persecutor who wants to possess him and therefore imprison him. When the victim feels the lack of his executioner, then he has a yearning, sick desire, as he puts the value of the other before his own value. It is a subversion of the inner order, a distortion of one's own identity. We feel lost in this condition, we are unrecognizable to ourselves, we are no longer us. It is said that seduction is subversive, because this type of sick seduction is placed on the side of evil, the other,has the power to make us touch the bottom, it is diabolical, in front of him our dignity is canceled, but this is sick love, is deadly dependence, which does not increase as the victim's regression is no longer the service of the ego and the victim is at the mercy of himself, abandoned, wounded, annihilated in his will, ensnared in a devouring phantasmatic passion , which affects the very perception of his dignity, this is a mortal charm, the charm of the abyss.

In the Christian tradition, we have the example of Satan who seduces Eve, because the ancients had already understood everything in their own way, Satan manipulates Eve in an attempt to subdue her, deceives her, deceives her to control her. In this situation, the plane of power dominates the plane of love and when this happens, we can speak of sick love.

F. Guzzardi

The Narcissist covert

The Wolves in sheep's clothing

2

Unlike open narcissists who show their narcissism and flaunt it nonchalantly, the covert narcissist is as if somehow sensed that showing the public their narcissism is not quite productive for them, it is not in their best interest and therefore it hides.

Precisely for this reason they are even more difficult to grasp, they are able to manipulate the people around them much better and they are much more dangerous for people who start a relationship with them.
The narcissist exhibits at least 5 of the following symptoms pervasively.

The first trait is, a grandiose sense of self, or an exaggerated sense of one's own importance.

The second is occupied by fantasies of unlimited success, of power over effects, over others, of beauty, of ideal love.

The third point, he believes he is special and unique and can only be understood by special people and or is overly concerned with seeking closeness and being associated with people of some very high status.

The fourth, requires excessive admiration compared to normal or its real value.

Fifth point, a strong feeling of their rights and faculties. Realistically convinced that other individuals or situations must meet his expectations.

Sixth, he takes advantage of others to achieve his own goals and feels no remorse.

Seventh point, which in my opinion is also one of the most, is always present toensure that a person is pathological narcissist, lack of empathy, does not notice, does not recognize or does not give importance to the feelings of others, does not want to identify with their desires. He often feels envy and is generally convinced that others feel envious of him / her.

Eight, He often feels envy and is generally convinced that others feel envious of him / her.

Nine, affective mode of predatory type, unbalanced power relations with littlepersonal commitment, wishes to receive more than what it gives.

These criteria were created some time ago, possibly today there are many more updates in the research, it is still an excellent guide to give an idea of a person with Narcissistic Personality Disorder. What transpires from these criteria is that we have an arrogant, manipulative person who imposes himself on others, who exploits others, without conscience, without remorse, who thinks only of himself, therefore completely selfish, who has only his own interests in mind, which demands too much of others.

All these characteristics are the characteristics of a classic narcissist but now let's see who the covert narcissist is.

The narcissist covert therefore, hides his narcissistic traits and hides them very well, to the point of often appearing the exact opposite of a narcissist. A covert is often confused with an dependent.He presents himself to the outside world as an extremely good and kind person, as a shy and introverted person, a person with something special but that society cannot understand because he is too far behind him. As a victim of the cruel world who does not understand it and does not and does not respect it. Often the covert narcissist, in his life, carries out activities that make him a pillar of society, very often voluntary work, social activities perhaps in charity or for the defense of the environment, for the defense of animal rights and other things similar. He finds himself at the center of this type of activity obviously surrounded by co-dependent people who are instead in those activities for genuine reasons. Be presented as a person of great ethics, who cannot understand why others are unable to reach this level of ethics, a person who gives a lot without receiving anything, in short, when you meet him you would say that you are dealing with a a person with a sensitive soul a generous and extremely empathetic person.

They are masters at feigning empathy, unlike classic overt narcissists who do not tolerate criticism at all, covert narcissists are extremely upset with criticism just like normal narcissists, only they hide their intolerance.

Another very interesting thing and that unlike the classic narcissists who never apologize or almost never, coverts learn very quickly that apologizing keeps them close to their victims and therefore often apologize they are never sincere excuses, but always a game in order to continue to use their victims.

A manipulative tactic that covert narcissists use a lot, are crying fits, existential crises and crises in general, in which they burst into tears of crying and self-pity. But, if you look very carefully, you notice that those are actually so much a game too, and if you pay close attention, you will notice that while they cry if they think you are not watching, they will check you to see your reaction.

Often the covert narcissist, in his life, carries out activities that make him a pillar of society, very often voluntary work, social activities perhaps in charity or for the defense of the environment, for the defense of animal rights and other things similar.

3

Five things about a narcissistic mother

You are evaluated for how you are perceived, not for who you are

3

Although we can consciously recognize the lack of love and our unhappiness within our family of origin, it is unlikely that we will be able to see the ways and behaviors that we have adopted to face and manage them.

It is much more likely that you will see your adult behaviors as deriving from your innate personalities rather than considering the various traits as answers learned within an environment that has formed us.
Many of your own ways of acting and reacting – could be fear of being rejected, difficulty in talking about yourself, panic when you are at the center of someone's attention, difficulty in trusting others, how he always blames himself when things go wrong – they are, in fact, attributable to those experiences he had in childhood.

The biggest effect on each daughter is her insecure attachment style which reflects both her shortcomings in managing emotions and her unconscious patterns of considering how people behave in relationships; having a mother full of narcissistic traits can lead to any of the three insecure styles that are anxious-worried, fearful-avoidant and contemptuous-avoidant.
Being raised by a mother full of narcissistic traits leaves a lasting influence on a daughter.

1 . **You are evaluated for how you are perceived, not for who you are.**

The mother full of narcissistic traits sees her children as nothing but extensions of herself, and she is therefore fully committed to ensuring that they reflect her personality and characteristics. He worries enormously about appearances and very little that children get results for what they actually did. The child who does not follow this program will become a scapegoat and ostracized.

2 . **Love is conditioned and can be reversed.**

What passes through love in the domain of the narcissistic mother is praise and attention, and both depend on the fact that the daughter continues to "reflect" the mother well, even in adulthood. Since this mother sees love as something to be earned, she feels perfectly comfortable revoking it if a daughter disappoints her. Of course, the daughter grows up believing that love is nothing more than a transaction that requires counterparts and, moreover, forces you to look over your shoulder.

3. To belong, you must respect the rules.

Since the narcissistic mother requires her children to present themselves as she imposes, bankruptcy is not acceptable. Many daughters understandably become very fearful of failure and, consequently, are unable to face challenges; they are aiming for low and safe goals. Others, intent on collecting the praises of their mothers, aim high and sometimes make it but, in the end, do not attribute to themselves what they have achieved or of which they have come into possession; outwardly winners, inside they feel false or cheating.

There are always "insiders" and "outsiders".

The world the child sees, is filtered from the mother's point of view; there are winners and losers, people who are within its special orbit, those who are outside who have no status and value.

The mother full of narcissistic traits, is with her favorite children, putting one child against the other, observing how each one works to attract attention. It is not surprising that the daughter/son, grows up believing that this is how the world works in general and that all relationships follow these same patterns. Do you think that one is always chosen to be part of the team, starting with that of the mother, or destined to remain outside it.

4. Verbal abuse is always to be expected and manipulation is the norm.

F. Guzzardi

All children assume that what happens in their home happens everywhere, and the daughter of a narcissistic mother is no different in this. For her it will usually be normal not only the behavior of the mother who puts one child against another, making it a scapegoat, designating winners and losers, but also the way in which she addresses her.

5. Nicknames, derision and manipulations are usually part of this mother's repertoire.

It is the way she keeps her children in line, and the daughter becomes unable to recognize verbal abuse. This predisposes her to consider these toxic behaviors normal in other relationships in her life, both as a young person and in adulthood.

It is not unusual for a daughter marginalized by a narcissistic-rich mother to end up with a lover or consort who treats her the same way. Until a girl tackles the behaviors determined by the mother's narcissism, even with the help of a therapist, this will continue to have a disastrous influence on her life, concludes the scholar.

4

God is dead

God is the belief, in an other-worldly that is metaphysical, it represents an escape from existence.

4

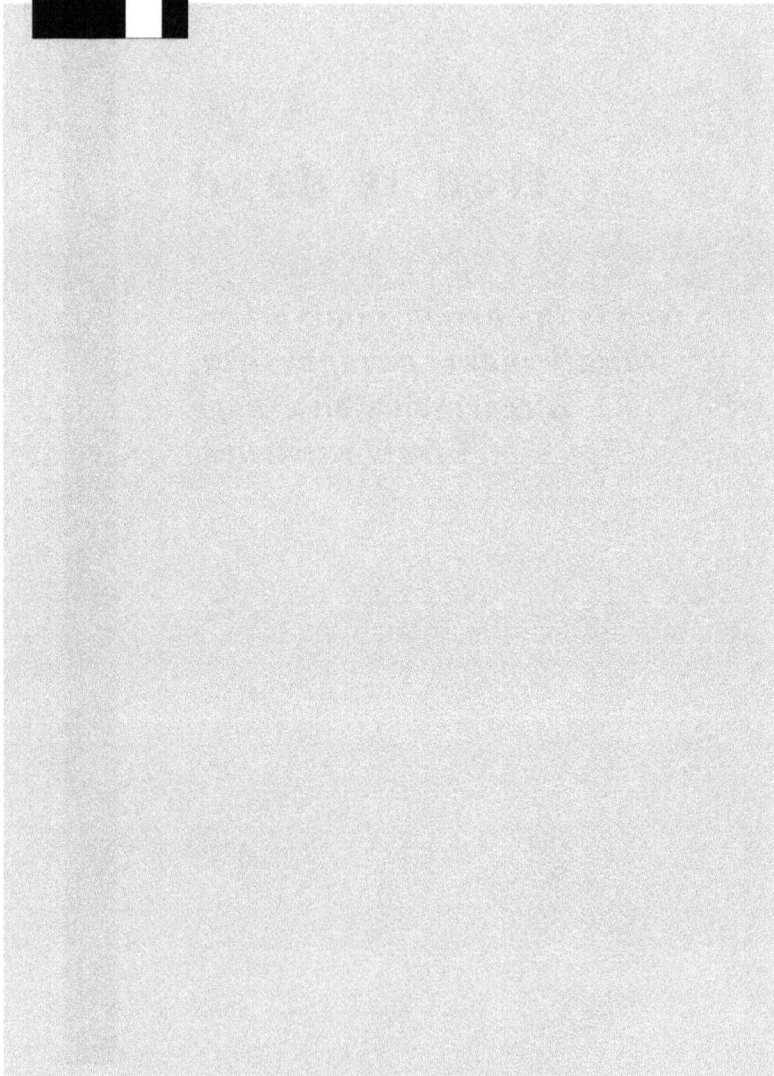

What is the death of God? Who is this God?

According to Nietzsche, God is our longest lie, God is the personification of all the various moral and religious certainties through which humanity has given a reassuring sense to the reigning chaos. God is the essence of all man-made beliefs to cope with the fear of the absence of logic, and therefore of something beneficial that guides everyone's life.

For Nietzsche, there is only one world, and this world is false, a cruel, contradictory and meaningless world. Therefore, we need the lie to overcome this reality, that is, to live moderately happy.

God is the belief, in an otherworldly that is metaphysical, it represents an escape from existence.

With the expression "God is dead," Nietzsche means the end of the certainties that have guided men but, the death of God, is not an event but something in progress, and is announced by the so-called "madman" that is the philosopher, while the rest of humanity is not yet fully aware of this truth that causes trauma, the trauma caused by God's death is the prelude to the advent of superman.

Only those who have become aware and accept that there are no more reassuring lies can be able to relate to reality and therefore plan their existence in a free way and beyond any metaphysical construction. The third phase of Nietzsche's philosophy opens precisely with the superman, the philosophical concept that is placed in the future and which corresponds to the idea of a new man, different from what we all know.

The characteristics of this superman are the acceptance of the intrinsic dimension of existence, the awareness of the death of God, and the end of certainties, the new man, remains faithful to the earth, remains faithful to his body, which are the the only realities in which to express one's essence.

The superman lives in the continuous, going beyond himself, he lives in creating, planning his existence in a free way and beyond any established scheme. In this, he is an artist, as he establishes a sense in the face of the chaos of the world and frees himself from the weight of time and the past. The superman is the one who has understood that it is he himself who gives meaning to life and makes his own the so-called "aristocratic morality" which says yes to life and therefore to the world. The superman is a disciple of Dionysus, since he accepts life in all its manifestations, in the pleasure of becoming understood as an alternation of life and death, of joy and pain.

This man faces life with a sort of courageous pessimism, and is capable of combining fatalism with trust and has freed himself from the worn concepts of good and evil, through an elitist indifference to ethical values that he considers dead. For the "other man" every moment is the center of his time of which he is always the protagonist, the eternal return, that is, the eternal repetition, in this context is the doctrine that Nietzsche puts into the new conception of the world, that is the present moment, must be lived spontaneously, without continuity with the past and with the future, because past and future are illusions, in fact every moment repeats itself identically in the past as in the future, like a die thrown to infinity, because time is infinite, it will give an infinite number of times the same numbers, as its choices are a infnite number.

In conclusion, the true "superman" is the one who no longer dances in chains but freely and with grace, as he is a free spirit in all senses. The moment that man lives is immense, it incorporates all its meaning in itself, its uniqueness has always generated a series of criticisms, a series of questions. One of the questions that has arisen in the history of criticism is the consideration of what the real Nietzsche is or what his real intent was and what he wanted to communicate in his works.

Empathetic animals

Sometimes I wonder what it must be like to feel empathy for others, t experience only emotions related to anger, fear, envy. Still, there is a very high percentage of people in the world that are almost totally empathetic. Sometimes I think that if there was a God or some other higher identity, it would surely be a totally empathy-free animal. It must be sad, pretend to love, pretend happiness, pretend emotion, embrace, mention a love you. Terrible, to give birth a child to prove that, we are equal to veryone, or to marry someone to hate. Hate all their family members by pretending to be the best of their children or brother, father or mother. It must be terrible, yet many of them live next to us, hey can be friends (fake) Wives or husbands (fake) or lovers.

If there was a God.

Sometimes I think that if there was a God, these people would be his children and that would also be natural, since God would not have empathy, they would also be the favorite children, in his image and likeness, isn't it also written in the Bible?

The anti – God

Here, this I think and terrifies me that it could happen to one of my children or even to one of my neighbors. What worse divine punishment (typical of the Gods) can exist if not that, of not feeling emotions towards others. That almost premonitory gift of feeling the other part of your world, of grasping the subtle inclinations of mood, feeling the pity and compassion without which there can be no understanding of the other. Being able to mitigate the sense of envy typical of the species, soften arrogance, mitigate anger, control fears. Empathy is the anti-God par excellence and this is why Narcisio assumes an attitude of Omnipotence, that is, he makes himself similar to God, totally devoid of empathy towards the rest of the world.

5

Toxic relationships

"You will experience this moment as extremely devastating, you will not be able to understand what just happened, a lightning bolt that just fell in your life".

5

F. Guzzardi

"The day before, he/she was sending you love letters, promising marriages and the next day you no longer exist, he/she tells me that " no longer loves me and that I no longer exist for him / her".

This seems like a drastic change but in reality it is only on the surface, this is not really the case, in fact, the narcissist has been preparing this moment for a long time behind your back, so long before that, I discard it in if it happened he has already started a whole phase of preparation.

At this point he has therefore created his point of support, for when he will reject you, most likely he/she is also already looking for another prey, another companion, another partner, already has a relationship with him / her and maybe he/she is already starting a phase of love bombing which preparing a whole circle of his, to which he/she can return, once he/she has lost your narcissistic supply.

However, you must understand that with a narcissist, a breakup is not simply the end of a relationship as it is for a healthy person.

In fact, the gap in the case of the narcissist does not have the objective of ending the relationship, because he / she would like to keep you at his disposal for the future in case he succeeds in attracting you again.

But in the reasoning in the narcissistic reasoning, the reason for this action is to annihilate you. So he will do it in the cruellest way possible, to create the greatest suffering possible, on purpose because in this way he will have restored his narcissistic fantasy. in fact when he sees you destroyed you no longer exist, therefore you are no longer a danger to his narcissistic fantasy. Up to now you were questioning him / her, so choose this moment when maybe you are extremely vulnerable, maybe you feel bad or you just got out of the hospital, just had a big loss, right now there will be a big fight, always because of your conflicts and myths and it will climb to a very high level, or then the relationship itself will put itself in an extremely vulnerable position and you are in that position and therefore it will cut you clean.

In this way, you are so overwhelmed by the shock factor and your already extremely vulnerable position that you will absolutely not have the strength to rebel while he / she will be able to get out without having to face his responsibility, in short, his narcissistic pain will go out. he is unharmed because he will have shown that you are the problem, that you are no longer a valid "prey", but something that no longer has any value and at the same time, a circle of prey has already been prepared which instead confer his self-narcissistic view again.

You will experience this moment as extremely devastating, you will not be able to understand what just happened, a lightning bolt that just fell in your life. Until the day before she had a partner who you thought was a fallen God, the next day you are faced with a monster who behaved in the worst possible way. You feel terrible, because you were already very weak, you were also in a very vulnerable position in the relationship and plus you just got completely cut off in the cruellest way possible.

But I want you to understand that if you take this moment to your advantage, if you understand and use it to wake up, to open, to evolve, to expand, to grow, this is also your blessing and not only that, you must also understand that when this moment comes when the narcissist has discarded you this is your victory."
"In reality this moment means that you are no longer a malleable person, that you are no longer a person who can be manipulated, harnessed, who can be stepped on. It means that you have become a person of integrity and that is why the narcissist has left you; because if he weren't, all those things, he would still be looking for you, so this is the moment when you are actually starting to blossom, to be the person that

you have always been inside of you and have never been able to have the courage to be. , contrary to what you are thinking, when it just happened, that is "oh my God I must have done something very serious" in reality nothing happened, you did nothing wrong and I assure you that the narcissist has absolutely not changed, he has simply changed scene, but he's exactly the same person as before.

He has learned absolutely nothing from your relationship, from the mistakes made with you, he is repeating his own play, certainly perfected but still always acting, with other people willing to play his game, contrary to appearances nothing has changed, it has not changed. nothing happened and you have done absolutely nothing wrong, indeed you have done something right, and that is precisely why he / she has gone, just because you have finally started not being a prey.

After all, your time has come to begin your path of healing, of inner growth, and finally, to reborn the person that you have truly always been and that you have never had the chance to fully become. Therefore the narcissist's moment of rejection, it was the beginning of your real life, your first step of victory and the beginning of the exploration of who you really are, and if you take this path I assure you that you will find within yourself strength, quality, love and compassion you never even imagined you had."

6

Heal your sexual trauma

The artificial cause that man must be a predator and must therefore always want sex, means that many sexually abused men are not taken seriously.

6

I will explain to you, why it is impossible to talk about sexuality without touching the social aspect. So let's start with this.

During our childhood, we are subjected to a whole range of emotional abuse and neglect of varying severity, and one of these types of abuse, the less discussed, is sexual abuse. One of the very characteristic things about sexual abuse, is that socially they tend to be different, male from female. When a girl grows up, basically in our culture, her sexuality is repressed in different ways, for example when the children are still in diapers and therefore are exploring their surrounding world, it can happen that their hands go precisely in the genital areas and therefore they feel that there are different sensations in those parts, in the case of females, what often happens, the parent who takes care of the child, tends to move the child's hand away from those areas, as if to mean something incorrect. On the other hand, in the case of male children, there is a tendency not to intervene.

As girls grow up, they tend to be ashamed and guilty of their sexuality, for example a girl who is turning into a woman and freely expresses her sexuality can be called a person of little value, simply because she chooses to expressing her sexuality or having sex for pleasure. Conversely, when a child grows up he is taught to become almost a sex creditor, having almost convince women to have sex with him. In many cultures, a man's worth is based on how much he is able to sexually conquer women. Obviously this creates a major social problem, on one hand, women who learn to repress their sexuality from childhood, on the other, men who become sex-hungry predators.

Thus begins a race of deficiency, of lack of sex that often leads the man to take refuge in compensatory behaviors to fill that void. So they turn either to porn, as a junk food of sex, or to prostitution, where there are often many women extremely abused and forced into sexual practices.

Men who use porn tend to enjoy less during sexual practice, this is precisely because most of the porn we see in circulation is of such a degrading level, and lacking in respect towards women. Then, when we are in a real situation, it is not enough to be stimulated a little but like junk food, when a person gets used to eating that, then the real food no longer tastes, because we get used to excess salty or sweet flavors.

All this, to get to our pathological narcissist who, predator and manipulator, very often exploits sexual trauma to create monographs. In the case of women for example, if a woman has suppressed her sexuality, the narcissist can play the role of liberator of this woman's sexuality, perhaps making her have particularly pleasant experiences or making her feel free from that point of view in order to then hook her. sexually or use this hook to control her life. But on the other hand, a female narcissist can exploit men's thirst for sex, and in fact many female narcissists tend to use sexual seduction to act as a hook, to bait men.

This violation continues and we even see it in the media as the woman's body and sexuality are used, as a tool. This causes many women to live with sexual trauma within them which can then be exploited by narcissists. The narcissist can take advantage of people's particular traumas.

In our culture, many women and children grow up with more or less serious sexual trauma because, as they grow up, the sexuality of girls and women is often violated both when they are children and later in adulthood.
The sexual limits of girls are constantly violated, by parents, relatives, classmates, friends, etc.
This violation continues and we even see it in the media as the woman's body and sexuality are used, as a tool. This causes many women to live with sexual traumas within themselves which can then be exploited by narcissists. This obviously applies to men who, precisely being in a state of sexual defciency and often strong gaps in self-esteem related to sex or another more serious trauma.

The artifcial cause that man must be a predator and must therefore always want sex means that many sexually abused men are not taken seriously.

Their use is not considered as such and is therefore repressed and this can then be exploited by any manipulators.

With that said how do we heal our sexual abuse?

Like all traumas, sexual abuse must also be healed by focusing not only on the emotions related to that aspect of us, but also on the body sensations, even in the intimate parts or emotions related to those areas.

Talk to an expert, you can go search on the internet, Google and you will find tons of experts and tons of pages that describe this topic with many details on how to use tools to heal our sexual aspect.

A nother reason why it is very important to heal this aspect of ours to take care of us is linked not only to our sexuality but also to our creativity, our desire, our pleasure. So our ability to be creative is also related to our sexual aspect. By repressing that aspect we repress a very important part of our life, also for this reason it is very important to go and heal, to work on ourselves.

7

The Real You

"When you lose your mind for someone, there, you are really yourself".

F. Guzzardi

W hen you lose your mind for someone, there, you are really yourself, it is the primordial energy that inhabits you, that energy that falls in love and never does it by chance, it is di cult to make a mistake. This is why the loves that involve us totally, are essential to our evolution, they are like the foundations of a house, they are your center, which is that something capable of sending away all doubts and that something capable of making us respond and give the answers we seek.

Who we are ?
We are an energy that governs our body !

I often hear people saying: " I have worked a lot on myself and now, I finally know myself ".
The soul is not something that lives in the time, the being that we are, is unknown to us, and does not want to trust to the arguments that often ruin all the beauty the life gives us. We must learn not to decide, we must know that the center of the emotional life is not something that belongs to us, it is not ours, it must not be judged by us.

A primordial energy that governs our body, that creates our being! In each of us there is an ancient, primordial man or woman, a primeval being, as the great sages knew, a being who lives in an underground bond, with all the things in the world.This bond manifests itself in dreams, in the encounters that are the substance of the Ancient man and woman who lives there, it is this primordial energy, which has the flavor of providence, comes on aid of us, and that is why we never fall in love by chance, because this providential energy takes care of us.

A sentence that we need to focus on is, I am myself when I make love; the "Ancient woman" knows what to do for us she knows where to take us, she knows which love is right for us; when there is involvement, when there is Eros, or passion, we enter this real Im and the loves in which we are involved are useful for

our evolution, they are just like the foundations of a house and are close to our essence. But if we want them to be truly useful, we must not make any decisions simply, we must accept and not work on ourselves, or ask ourselves if a love is good or not; is something that does not know anything and is deleterious. This deeply, disturbs the soul and does not need your approval, but it needs our
silence.

The artistic eyes of the unconscious

Love, is something that strips, empties the slogan, overturns it, subverts it.

8

F. Guzzardi

The emotional involvement! Or rather, the loving feeling, in fact it is the loving feeling that manages to transform people. The feeling, however, is nourished by desire ... let's say right away that no psychotherapist will be able to save us, but will be able to animate our life with desire, activating the desire contained in our biography.

The activation of this desire can only take place thanks to an example. We therefore need a testimony of what it means to live, on the one hand lack, and on the other desire. Our suffering arises from an intoxication of ideas, in practice what we cannot manage is the experience of failure, for which every obstacle is removed as imperfection disturbs the ideal image we have of us.

A bit like being pushed towards success but not being able to endure failure. This means that the error is experienced not only as a defeat but also as a catastrophic fall and the fall is not accepted.

But living in the name of feeling, above all means accepting the possibility of failure, which is also the time of loss and mourning or if you want it is the time of doubt.

Therefore, the path of psychological transformation is the path of failure, and in this path, there is always a fall from a horse, or an encounter with the earth, face to face with the hard spirit of the Real. So in order for there to be an encounter with oneself, and therefore with one's own truth, it is necessary to get lost, it is necessary to fail, whoever has never been lost does not know what it means to find oneself.

One thing that allows metamorphosis, is love, but what are the enemies of love? The enemies of love are the limiters, the dogmatism that makes us too full of ideas, makes us saturated with concepts."

Love, is something that strips, empties the slogan, overturns it, subverts it. But when we are full of words and we use them compulsively one after the other, the words lose their meaning because they flaunt a false superiority.

L ove, overcomes these limits. Many of us don't know how to use the language of the unconscious, we don't understand it, we are limited and more generally we don't even understand others, so we suffer.
It is a matter of developing this precious ability and the first subversive step is to open the mind to the encounter, which is always an encounter with the stranger who dwells within ourselves. An encounter with the otherness present within us. When this encounter becomes a relationship, it evokes a symbolic language.

The meeting makes you dream and is not static, this is an opening movement and then everything starts to change because we see with artistic eyes. But when we are full of words and we use them compulsively one after the other, the words lose their meaning because they flaunt a false superiority.

The unconscious is an artist, it is subversive, the unconscious is the place of an opening, that is, of a new possibility and at the same time an ancient possibility, always written, which calls the subject to an unconscious mission.

It is the witness of what we would like to be and what can be. We must grasp the artistic ability of the unconscious and therefore its ability to create new projects, new visions to change ourselves.

The law of attraction

We all know that a magnet attracts objects but it can also repel depending on the magnetic polarity.

9

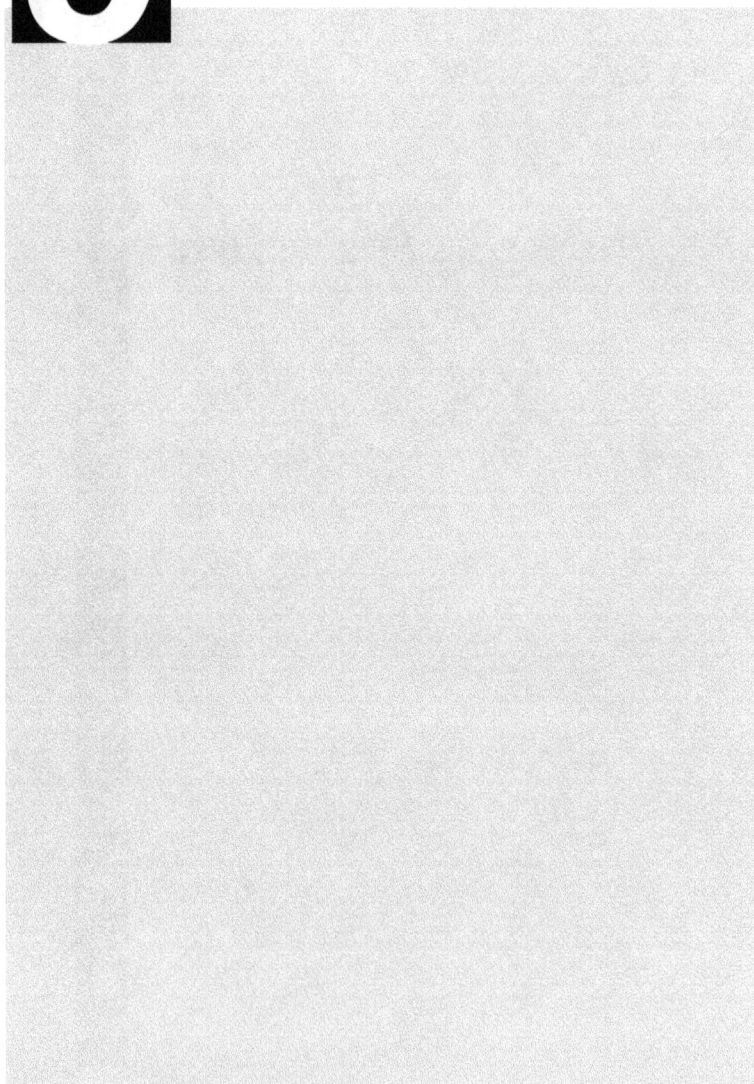

The law of attraction state that your thoughts come true. That is, that you are able to attract what you are thinking about. If you focus enough on your desire for example, the desire to get rich, sooner or later this will happen, because youare attracting wealth..The phases of the law of attraction are essentially three, asking, believing and then receiving.

Those who apply the law of attraction do at least two things: ask, that is, define a goal clearly and believe, that is, keep a high focus on this goal.
If you know what you want and if you know when you want it and how you intend to get it, you have just taken the first concrete step to make your dream come true. If we don't act consistently and consistently, our dreams will remain nothing but money, as Steve Jobs says.

We are here to leave a trace, so it is the ability to attract into our lives, whatever we desire, both positive and negative, through the power of our thoughts.

We all know that a magnet attracts objects but it can also repel depending on the magnetic polarity. If we think of ourselves as a kind of human magnet, we understand that we exert a force through thoughts.
Basically we act as human magnets, sending their thoughts and emotions outward, and in this way we exert a force that is able to change the course of our events.

Unfortunately, many of us don't realize the potential that's locked away in our minds and let our desires and emotions negatively control their lives when instead they may be able to create the future they want. the field of quantum physics in recent years has helped shed light on the incredible impact that the power of the mind has on our lives and the universe.

This idea is being explored by the scientific community. The greater the understanding of how significant is the role of the mind in shaping our lives, and the world around us. Quantum physics is a branch of physics, which deals with the study of quanta.

When we remain in a state of receptivity and therefore of gratitude, particular patterns of the mind emerge which increase the so-called positive vibes that people want to be around us and join us. In that state of harmony, this phenomenon also extends to other sensory mechanisms. When we feel something instinctively, which is therefore dictated by our inner voice, or when we visualize a hypothetical scenario in our mind, it is, as if we are experiencing it and therefore, we are attracting that condition, that positive experience. While when a person remains passive, letting himself be carried away by events and accepting whatever is offered to him, he falls prey to the chaos of nature.

Of course, the way we have been raised and educated and therefore our past our mental superstructures our mental patterns and the people around us all play a key role in shaping our mental patterns. All this seems simple at first glance, but many people have no idea what they really want, because we must first, as I said before, determine what our desires are, what exactly we want. It is important to create a clear mental picture of our desire by going into the smallest details, having and cultivating a vision.

To do this we must first transform all negative statements into positive statements, a negative statement, for example, is: "I will never be able to pay off my debts", I can reverse this statement and I can say: "I will have the necessary money to repay all debts ".

The law of attraction is very sensitive to our positive feelings, the person who constantly sees the glass half empty will always be submerged in negativity.

F. Guzzardi

Negative and helpless words like "I can't, I can't, I shouldn't, I don't deserve," should be avoided. Because they strip us of our ability to manifest the life we really want to live.

We are therefore the creators of our psychological universe, and what we say will become our reality. If I say something like, "I'm overweight," I should try to turn that statement into a more positive statement, like," I'm getting healthier and with each passing day, I'm getting closer to my ideal weight.

Words are the paint with which we paint reality, that's why we should choose our words very carefully, with wisdom and positivity, to create a reality that is good for us and for the people around us. We should start with the little things, for example a typical exercise in the law of attraction is today I want to see something purple, if we say this sentence to ourselves and then visualize the color purple. You will be amazed to see how much this exercise works, because once you have visualized the purple color you will happen in the day to see objects that have precisely this color. Once you are familiar with the concept of the law of attraction, go step by step and manifest increasingly complex ideas and concepts.

10

Mandala

Nothing is permanent

10

F. Guzzardi

We ever wondered, why we're not happy? The first answer, the one that emerges immediately and spontaneously, will be: "I am unhappy because I am not well in the reality in which I live", and immediately afterwards someone might add: "I am not happy only because I am unlucky".

But how many people will have the courage to ask themselves: if it is perhaps up to me? We observe a Buddhist sage who constructs a Mandala, that set of figures, symbols, drawings that represent the deepest part of the psyche. Mandala means magic circle. This Buddhist master takes months and even years to silently arrange the colored powders, within a pattern of emblematic signs. But when he has finished it, with a breath or a gesture of the hand, he dissolves it or does not protect it from the wind that sooner or later will dissolve it.

This is to symbolically say that, in life, nothing is permanent.But this is also a way to explain to oneself and to those who look at us that, it is not necessary to become attached to a person or to become attached to an object, not even to something that I had created with so much fatigue. It is not even useful or beneficial to become attached to our ego, that is, to our way of being, to our way of acting; so whenever the death of something occurs, a rebirth arises, in the one who created that thing.

Our unhappiness begins there, where we persist in sticking to the dead pattern. We must begin to think gently about our life, as if it were a Mandala, as if it were a drawing of dust that is now there but in a moment it could vanish, it is precisely in this ability to live in a state of perennial transit, in this conscious instability that lies the secret of happiness which then coincides with the secret of self-esteem."

We are constantly looking for an explanation, a logic that explains past events and people we have met in our life, we are always looking for a reason and we ask ourselves why we have not been able to do better?

We are obsessed with the control of reason, we are obsessed with obtaining an explanation that puts us safe from future suffering but, let's stop and think. Let's start by saying that if a person enters our life, that is the right person! In the psyche there is no chance, nothing happens by chance and every person who goes through our life does it to teach us something, for better or for worse, and does it to favor our evolution. Everything that happens to us makes sense, it has an ultimate purpose that is important to grasp, so whenever we feel something, that is the right moment.

It means that we are ready to welcome something new in our life, the new will begin and in the same way what is finished must be left and we must proceed enriched with the teaching acquired.

If I meet a person along my path, this is because I chose to walk that path, I did it because I liked it, therefore, let's say, subconsciously, I will meet people who have to do with my choice, and it makes no sense to mull over why some decisions have led us, off course, it will mean that I have simply experienced what it does for me and what it does not do for me, I have become aware of where I can, where I want to go, and it is in that direction that our thoughts and energies must be concentrated, the past cannot be changed and it is not possible to return to feel good as if by magic if we have not first learned what made us feel bad and we have not treasured that experience. If we do learn from our experience, we will be able to change. Our responsibility is to recognize the particularity of our life, desire, in particular, and this desire has a name, a face and a voice, waiting to be discovered.

THE RIGHT PERSONNE

We invest a lot of energy in looking for the right person with whom to share our life and according to common sense the right person, that is, the soul mate is the one who shares with us the values and goals of life. But to recognize the right person we should first learn to know ourselves, our deepest desires and before choosing we should feel we are the right person, that is, we should be in harmony with ourselves accepting ourselves for what we are, then it will appear. Some wait for the right person with the pretense that he can improve their life by filling the void outside. But if you know who you are, you will automatically know what you want. On the contrary, the right person will find you if you live in peace with yourself, in harmony with your inner world, you will have no difficulty in forming authentic relationships and cultivating relationships.

If, on the other hand, you have unresolved conflicts, if you do not live in harmony with your internal world and drag along needs, others will have news of these unmet needs and you will tend to be a victim of the classic narcissist on duty, which will represent the attempt to fix something wrong and a bitter disappointment will soon come because in this case, one of the components of the couple finds in the other the reinforcement of the false representation that he has of himself, and everything becomes an obligation of the couple relationship, not the dreams, but the potential. To understand from the first moments if is the right person you have to be on peace with yourself, this is the reason why many relationships tend to focus on their expectations, forgetting to ask what can make you happy.

The key to a happy relationship is the ability to accept diversity. Relationships with others are necessary because we are not satisfed with our dreams. The sexual revolution, becoming sexy is the cultural revolution of the last decades,has transformed feelings into objects of consumption. .

Today satisfaction is promoted, indeed oneself, continuously looking for a strong emotion in the absence of which one calls back, breakfast with the internet, the choice of partner becomes limited and how satisfed we are with the person we love the myth of infinite choice will tell us that somewhere in the world there is a better person waiting for us perhaps just one click away. Then we add that cinema and television present love to us in a very difficult way to achieve, increasing a reason for dissatisfaction.Whenever we build a relationship with others we must know that the relationship is a kind of tool that allows us to discern what without the other we would not have seen in ourselves, therefore each new relationship is like a new conversation with oneself.

Because it puts us on our trail, arouses curiosity around ourselves, makes us feel our own presence. I love you is an invitation to get out of yourself and get moving. But to search, you need to track down who frst walked that stretch of road, I love you means that that person can be you and that your path is full of achievements, of changes. It means that it is a journey made up of meetings.

What the other proposes by telling us I love you is an adventurous and fascinating journey through our inner labyrinth, the promise of living together experiences that make us grow. I love you is a path, an entrance that will lead us to the inner center, in the heart of the labyrinth, where we will have a transformative experience, and then return to the world renewed.

I love you

Loving is like being drunk and delusional but in contact with the sacred

F. Guzzardi

I n real life, it happens that things are not simply right or wrong, there are not only black and white, the truth in a meeting is nuanced, and relational. To enter into a relationship you need to let go of something of yourself, and it is not always like chatting on a computer because the other has his own labyrinth, a living space that exposes us to risks. The understanding of the other is made up of many tests that lead to one's inner center, the heart of the "I love you" is the seat of the mystery, if we do not face this journey, we would never have the opportunity to reach the truest part of the our being and I love you is a powerful push to enter the spirit.

"It is a flight! Man has always dreamed of flying, at the bottom of each of us, there is a little Icarus who looks up and wants freedom but to experience this transgression in a fruitful way we also need some rules. It takes thought, feeling, intuition, action. Each of us is looking for our promised land and in this search, we don't need to ask ourselves if our romantic relationship is right or wrong because it doesn't matter, what really matters and what happens to us while we drink it, how we change and how we grow, the crime that most often we commit, is not to see our true value, so we fly low, we are satisfied with what we think we are but, we are much more than that and we do not know, we do not know until we meet a person other than others, which spurs us to imagine new things and gives us the courage to look within. He tells us I love you.

In front of the "I love you," we are taken by restlessness, by fear, but fear is the beginning of the search, fear is the beginning of our psychology, love excites fear, we are afraid of loving because the other it is like a labyrinth, it is an initiatory path that leads to our inner center, where we can harmonically reunite ourselves.

Loving is like being drunk and delusional but in contact with the sacred, in a mystical condition thanks to which the fictitious identification is abandoned, to know the true object of our desire which is called dispossession of the ego in favor of a new psychic totality but, this is a real practice of death, I love you and also know how to die, to know how to be born again of desire. At this point for the ego, it is time to re-emerge on the surface but, by now, it has learned to descend to die and to be reborn as well as ever.

The borderline paradox

F. Guzzardi

There is a trend, today's relationships are often destructive and have one common feature, breaking them can be very difficult. In fact, even when the love has long since ended, one of the two partners can decide to continue the relationship because he is afraid of the reactions of the other, which can even reach threats or suicide attempts. Or the classic vendettas, retaliation. To avoid all this, it is advisable to break the relationship gradually and cautiously, making the relationship cool, diluting the meetings and if possible it should be made sure that it is the most problematic partner, to break away but without making him feel rejected.

In the relationship with a borderline, you have the feeling of being with two different people, a devil and an Angel who alternate suddenly and in an unpredictable way, from their point of view the other has gone mad and has become another person, a sour, angry, intolerant person, always ready to reproach something while before he was a sweet and in love person.

I hate you just becouse you love me

The borderline pathology involves a difficulty in regulating emotions and in particular negative emotions. It is like being without skin, therefore everything is experienced in an amplified way and with an unbearable intensity. For example, a small inattention on the part of the partner is perceived as a devastating abandonment, capable of generating strong feelings of despair.

The borderline can be summarized in this expression: "I hate you just because you love me", this is one of the strangest experiences found in relationships, which reciprocates love and attention, which it receives with hatred and contempt and it is a very common experience among problematic couples today, to reciprocate affection by becoming cruel. Sometimes we fall in love with abusive and ineffective people but we must never forget that at the base of certain behaviors that seem motivated only by gratuitous malice, there is a deep feeling, the whole world of the border is characterized by chronic feelings of emptiness and of worthlessness and depression. On a subconscious level, the borderline considers itself unworthy of love, unworthy of having any good things in life and that is why it becomes self- destructive and hurts those who love it, therefore it destroys all that good things can happen.

Observing the interaction between a border and his partner, we are baffled by the mood swings and his sudden changes of opinion; one day he says one thing and the next day he says the opposite. Or it promises something and does the exact opposite, so we don't know what to believe. The ego of the borderline is fragile and poorly integrated, therefore the subject is unaware of his many inconsistencies and contradictions in his behavior that do not depend on hypocrisy, as it might seem to an external observer but depend on the splitting of the ego and therefore on the inability to reflect on oneself. If confronted with his contradictions, the borderline reacts by trivializing or worse still, going into a rage and taking the offensive.

This happens, because criticism is perceived as devastating attacks. The borderline people live in a condition that resembles adolescence in some respects, which is a tumultuous phase, characterized by restlessness, identity crises and existential crises.

Basically they are individuals who don't know what they want to do with their life and don't know who they want to be. There is a lot of psychological instability which translates into a vital path characterized by continuous ups and downs and frequent changes in work and friendships.

People with this problem start 1000 projects with great enthusiasm and then abandon the frst difficulty; however, before making a diagnosis, we must not forget that, a behavior cannot be evaluated regardless of the context in which it occurs, and we must take into account that, the same symptom can present itself in very different personality structures.

Therefore a symptom does not the diagnosis, it is also good to remember that the diagnosis is not so much a list of symptoms as an overview of the personality, which explains how that particular person works in life, or what are his fears, his weaknesses, his resources, he explains to us what his defense mechanisms are and therefore his lifestyle, including maladaptive behaviors that manifest themselves in a pervasive and therefore in an inflexible permanent way, involving the cognitive sphere, the affective sphere and the relational sphere. Furthermore, we are in the presence of a personality disorder, this does not manifest itself only in the couple but the personality disorder is pervasive and this means that it manifests itself in most situations, not only with the partner but also with colleagues, neighbors, with family or friends even if the worst part will emerge from the intimate relationship.

Now, the end of a problematic relationship can leave deep wounds that can take a very long time to heal and you can feel devastated by the end of the relationship, failing to accept how what once seemed to be great love can ending so badly for no defnite reason and the partner who until the day before loved each other madly becomes inexplicably resentful and begins to detach emotionally by claiming that they are no longer in love.

In a relationship with a person suffering from borderline personality syndrome, these dynamics are common, yet giving up this painful relationship can be very, very diffcult. Rationally, the partner of the borderline clearly realizes that leaving would be the best solution but his emotional attachment remains very strong, also because there is no valid understanding of the pathology and therefore it is not possible to correctly read emotions and behaviors. "F. Guzzardi

Why do we always choose the wrong person in relationships?

We will call the first mechanism "completion," this mechanism implies that an emotional relationship can begin when we have intuited from our partner the characteristics that could complement us, that is, we feel attracted to precisely those personality characteristics that we believe our partner has and that we think we don't have. But choosing a partner based on this belief, is not wise and leads to bad relationships.

The second mechanism is the projection, according to which the partner we have chosen, allows us to strip ourselves of certain qualities by attributing them to her, therefore, the other becomes the dustbin that gives us the possibility to finally get rid of our psychic garbage. In this case the choice of the person to love will be conditioned by the projection, and this time too it will not be a wise choice.

T he third mechanism that favors a bad relationship, is that of reparation, that is, the other has such characteristics that being with him or her, makes us rethink the way in which we have been treated in the primary relationships, which are those with our parents; therefore the other offers us the opportunity to relive them and to repair them if they were not satisfactory. But even then it won't be a good choice.

Behind all these bad choices is a prejudice that goes like this: Facing life alone is a difficult thing and therefore, if I can find someone who heals my wounds or fills my shortcomings or someone I can project them onto, maybe together with this someone, we can function better. However, this is an erroneous belief, the consequence of this belief is that the relationship does not last long because it is based on an unrealistic vision of the other."

"This illusion is characterized by a rigid set of personality traits. In the diagnoses that are made in psychiatry there is a grouping of pathologies that encompasses all those rather rigid personalities marked by a strong emphasis on emotions, namely the histrionics, the borderline, the anti-social and the narcissist.

Let's try schematically to make some distinctions

The histrionic, is distinguished by an excessive affectivity, by a sort of theatricality and therefore a very explicit life Swede. This trait is often diagnosed in narcissistic women, the type who talks about her problems and demands that the other take care of her problems and will adapt to any request as long as the other is willing to give unconditional love in return.

The way of speaking of the histrionic is with a certain emphasis, it shows an exaggerated pathos, so much so that one often gets the impression of being in front of an actress, whatever we say, she will relaunch with the story of something more serious, of more exaggerated and dramatic than what we said. This will be enough to fascinate the other thanks also to the marked seductive skills and the eroticization of the relationship.

Maintaining an impeccable physical appearance, is an indispensable requirement for the histrionic who is often brilliant, intelligent, and gives the impression of knowing how to have fun with lightness and enthusiasm. The problem is that in the long run it tends to be excessively demanding and complaining, to the point of inducing the partner to run away. Often histrionic women look for men unlike them who know how to be rational because, by this type of men they feel protected, guided.

Borderline

In addition to the histrionic, we have the borderline, which stands out for its fears of abandonment, then for the emotional instability, feelings of emptiness, intense anger and the urge to lead an uncontrolled life. The relationship that the borderline proposes is made of rapid idealization and rapid devaluations that make it irremediably unstable, in fact the relationship precipitates because the two partners are unable to handle the overwhelming emotions that arise from the relationship. The core of this suffering and the fear of being abandoned are sometimes small daily gestures to which anyone would give little value that instead the borderline amplifies by experiencing them as signs of abandonment. In practice and continuously tested at all times, in every way and by any means. Until at a certain point, the other gets tired, is deprived of all energy, and in an attempt to protect himself, he moves away, then confirming in the borderline his fear of being abandoned.

Narcissist

But the most discussed personality of all, especially in recent times, is the narcissist. The difference between the narcissistic and the borderline condition derives from the fact that the narcissist has a grandiose self that is more integrated and structured but is still a pathological self that at any moment runs the risk of being invalidated. To protect this grandiose image of himself and to try to defend himself, he/she is forced to implement a series of strategies to maintain an emotional distance from others who become objects of anger and devaluation. The narcissist also has to deal with feelings of inferiority that are generated by a sadistic superego and then has to deal with a strong need to be reassured, hence the constant need to have a narcissistic supply deep feeling of envy towards others who are also saviors, because they are able to guarantee effective supplies and therefore confirmations, esteem and trust.

But they also become objects of anger, objects of aggression and hatred, because others are experienced as rivals. "Given these premises, it is understandable why the narcissist establishes a parasitic type relationship centered on the exploitation of the other. The other is used to support the grandiose self-image and to discharge frustrations. As a gift from the super ego, in the case of narcissistic parents, children can have several functions, for example, allowing the parent to strut his offspring: " Look what beautiful children I have generated " ! Or they can guarantee him a socially desirable image.

In general, outside the home, the narcissist changes personality and behavior, and is capable of transforming himself into the opposite of what he/she appears at home. At home, the narcissist does not have to show the best part of himself, therefore in front of strangers the narcissist will wear the mask of the caring mother or the impeccable father, smiling, attentive to the needs of the children and always ready to sacrifice himself for them. But this only adds to the family drama of

F. Guzzardi

these children who are still young and therefore are led to act like their parents to demonstrate to the public that they have received an impeccable education.

The golden Children

However, when the children grow up, the danger of confrontation between parents and children arises and things start to get complicated. Because the children reveal their first needs for autonomy and identification, perhaps choosing a university or professional path that the narcissistic parent does not approve of as he feels threatened by it. Thus this exemplary mother begins to crush children through ferocious accusations, through devaluations, in such a way that the children are not able to tarnish the grandiose image of a sort of despotic queen. Therefore, the children are constantly put in competition through continuous comparisons, generally a golden child is elected and then a scapegoat. The golden child and the idealized extension of the mother, that is, he is the chosen one, the one who is destined for great awards and honors. To this child, everything is allowed, family life basically revolves around the needs of the golden child and his wishes. This child gets the semblance of being loved and in return sacrifices himself on the altar of the narcissistic mother.

Sometimes, and being the golden child an older brother, he ends up abusing the younger brother who becomes the scapegoat, the scapegoat functions as a container of psychic garbage that the narcissistic parent cannot accept to keep within himself and therefore on this child is constantly deposited all the parts of the parent Narcissus that he cannot accept in himself. This child will often be incapable, it will be ugly, it will be the least intelligent child, it will be the too introverted, too extroverted child or the boring, inadequate, awkward child, someone to be ashamed of.

The scapegoat Child

The scapegoat child will be someone to be isolated and disowned as soon as possible, as he is the bearer of that defect that alters the presumed perfection of the narcissistic parent and therefore of the family to which he belongs. Not infrequently, the son who is the scapegoat is the frst to leave the family unit and this obviously happens not as a result of a physiological and healthy process of release from the family of origin but, as a result of a ferocious expulsion from the nucleus which forces the son to fee..

What unites all the children of narcissistic parents, whether they are golden children or scapegoats, is that, these children are sadly alone, these children in fact cannot ally themselves with their parents, they know how much the following rule applies in these families : If a narcissistic parent and especially if he is a perverse narcissist, the other parent is under the thumb, then the children will grow up alone, suffering in silence;

The perverse narcissistic mother succeeds in this intent by manipulating and mystifying others and subjecting them to gaslighting and then to smear campaigns. Typically they devalue the husband, and they also do it in front of the children, by doing so the narcissistic mother will teach the male child above all that devaluing and minimizing the merits of the father or brother and of all the men he will know in his life, is perfectly a fact normal, that's why we must recognize a perverse narcissist and not fall into the trap of emotional dependence.

The true love
Now, true love, be it parental or love within the couple relationship, exists but it can be called love only if there is a reciprocal bond, only if there is reciprocity! If reciprocity is lacking by defnition, it is a relationship that is born asymmetrical, that is, with the aim of saving the weaker person, it is compromised and here we go back to the speech we made at the beginning but, the problem increases when, as in the case of narcissist, because the narcissist hardly admits that he/she is the cause of the problems, and even more rarely, admits

that she has problems.

The narcissist learns from an early age to conceal, the core of his problem consists precisely in the inability to know oneself and to take contact with his most vulnerable part. Then his entire life will be aimed at unconsciously obtaining that compensation which is known as the narcissistic supply that the narcissist will search in a spasmodic way,finding it every time in the beautiful objects he will love to surround himself with, everything must be amazing and the greater it is to fill the void left by that family who, did not know how to love him, to the end, amazing things will be needed.

There will be a need for men willing to annihilate themselves in the name of unconditional love and endlesslove.

Finally, the narcissist shows little empathy, has a grandiosity and an arrogant attitude, a tendency to get bored easily, exploits and manipulates others to obtain confirmation of his value that is intimately perceived as lacking. In principle they are not able to establish a true bond of attachment which, in most cases is simply finished artfully, so it is a fiction, a fiction to obtain the confirmations that the narcissist needs. The narcissist often chooses an addictive partner, an adoring and condescending partner but, this partner, for its part, is able to make the other feel important, makes him feel strong and competent, but in the hope of obtaining psychological support in return and attention to one's most intimate needs.

They give life to a relational dance which very often leads to massacre, as the addicted person asks the narcissist for the love and support, that the narcissist will never be able to give, due to his disorder.

12

Narcissism VS Borderline

But what do the borderline and narcissist have in common?

F. Guzzardi

Both destabilize and confuse their partners with contradictory, hardly understandable behavior. Those who fall in love with them continually receive a double message: I love you and I hate you, I love you but I don't want a story, I want to be with you but I can't, which makes it difficult to know what to expect and above all how to behave.

Both the borderline and the narcissist have an insecure attitude that prevents trust in the partner, with the tendency to read his behavior in a negative key, even seeing him with an enemy or as someone who is not sincere towards them, who therefore does not he loves but wants to take advantage of them. Therefore, precisely because they do not trust, they are unable to accept that they need the other and never abandon themselves completely.

The feeling

Another problem they have in common is the inability to form a stable and relatively objective concept of the partner, which is idealized and immediately afterwards devalued.

Both the borderline and the narcissus are very vulnerable, it takes nothing to hurt them and when they feel hurt they react by devaluing and attacking or closing themselves in an icy silence.
It is not uncommon to hear of your partner one day as the wonderful man you would like to marry and the next day as a monster you can run away from. This happens because both narcissistic and borderline think in black and white according to the law of all or nothing and it takes very little to go from stars to rags.

Intimacy

For them it is a problem because intimacy is able to awaken the childhood experiences of humiliation and abandonment. For this reason, they cannot stay close to someone for too long, but moments of warmth and moments of coldness alternate in the relationship. They get hot when their partner moves away and cool when they feel too close.

Unfortunately, these dynamics do not change over time, the relationship does not grow even after many years but remains fragile at risk of sudden breakdown. Another aspect that unites the two disorders, is the tendency to manipulate therefore intolerance to criticism and the inability to have constructive discussions.

Differences

What a borderline wants from a relationship is very different from what the narcissist seeks.
Both were deeply injured in childhood, albeit in different ways. The wounds are deeper in the borderline, whose pathology is related to childhood experiences of abuse and mistreatment while the wounds are less evident in the narcissist who has been an idolized and spoiled but emotionally neglected child.

Both seek a reparative experience in love. In practice, the borderline seeks an absolute and total feeling, wants a symbiotic relationship with a person who loves him unconditionally and who, thanks to the power of love, can save him from his black holes and inner torments.

The problem is that when he finds someone who loves him madly, he can't trust him and feels the need to test the strength of the relationship, to the point of destroying it. The borderline has a disorganized type of attachment that is, he is in desperate need of love but the more love he receives the less he is able to appreciate it. The narcissist, on the other hand, is not looking for love but someone who can soothe his deep insecurity that he hides behind a brilliant appearance,

F. Guzzardi

enhancing his image and strengthening his self-esteem. It must be remembered that, in love, narcissists are guided by rationality and calculation rather than by the heart and are unlikely to commit to someone if the relationship does not bring them social advantages or economic, sexual or professional advantages or makes their life more comfortable. . If the partner does not meet the requirements in terms of their status or even physical requirements, they leave it.

To give an example, a narcissistic woman will not even look for a while at a man who does not have the desirable economic situation for how many human qualities he may have, vice versa he will tend to choose a socially affirmed partner even if perhaps there is not a great understanding.

The choice of the narcissist falls on socially desirable partners who have something out of the ordinary such as for example the man full of money with the big car or with friends or if it is a man he will choose the girl who looks like a model possibly much more. young of him who makes all men turn as he passes by as well as improving his image in the eyes of others and therefore in front of himself.

The ideal partner for a narcissist is an undemanding partner from an emotional point of view, because he is a partner willing to sacrifice his needs in favor of those of the Narcissus and therefore able to offer continuous confirmations, making him feel admired, desired and special. But even if the Narcissus finds a partner or a partner with all the right requirements and gets to the point of marrying him, the relationship remains superficial even after many years of life as a couple, moreover the Narcissus will remain in love only as long as the relationship remains exciting and able to satisfy the needs of narcissistic confirmation.
The relationship with the borderline, on the other hand, is rather a tormented and stormy relationship. Being with a person with this disorder means going from hatred to love without many middle ground and in an unmotivated and sudden way.

Borderlines have an innate difficulty in regulating emotions that causes them to experience very intense emotions, which they cannot control. When they love, they love madly, when they get angry their fury is destructive, when they want you, their desire is all-consuming. The narcissist, on the other hand, is not in touch with his emotional world, emotions frighten him, which is why he tends to control them.

Feel empty

Narcissists feel empty, cannot feel emotions, and are easily bored as a couple once the enthusiasm of the early days is overcome.

Now, if we focus on the experiences of the respective partners, The narcissist detaches from the borderline, we realize that it is a very different experience. The borderline partner will feel very loved at some times and intensely hated at others. The partner of the narcissist, on the other hand, will always feel insecure about the affection and devotion of the beloved, feeling that he must always be at his best in order to maintain his interest. Many daffodils voluntarily keep their mate on the rope, giving him little confirmation of their affection. This is a relational strategy to have power over the relationship.

The Narcissus who has avoidant attachment because he has a negative view of relationships, fears that if the partner knew how important it is to him or her they would use this awareness to control, dominate and exploit him. Then there is another very important difference between borderline narcissus, the borderline has a symbiotic relationship while the narcissus is an independent type. Being with a borderline means experiencing an exhausting back and forth in which honeymoon moments alternate with sudden and unmotivated breakups that are bound to increase as the relationship progresses.

Symbiotic relationship

F. Guzzardi

At the beginning the borderline tends to establish a symbiotic relationship, idyll and love with the partner, which excludes the rest of the world but the symbiosis is short-lived, usually lasts a few weeks and the borderline, in love until the day before, from point to point white can interrupt the date by telling his partner that he is no longer in love and that he has never loved him, only to retrace his steps after some time with a renewed feeling.

But even this parenthesis will not last and will be followed by other detachments that over time will become longer and longer until the relationship is completely worn down while the borderline feels the need to enter and exit the relationship and therefore to build, to destroy everything and then return to build, the Narcissus who has a more structured and more consistent personality than the couple has a different modality, even if both find it difficult to sustain a prolonged intimacy and often sex becomes the only form of intimacy that the daffodils can access, the narcissist is not symbiotic indeed, with him there will hardly be a us and is rather centered on himself and on his commitments, his interests, he behaves like a single person without taking into account the wishes and needs of his partner who he sees rather as whims or attempts to change it.

When the narcissist is taken up with his plans, he will forget about the partner, demanding however, understanding and unconditional availability. Moral of the matter, the borderline and the narcissist are too hurt and hurt to be able to truly love. They love only to the extent that the other can satisfy their needs and make them feel good about themselves.

13

The 6 phases
of Emotional
dependence

*"There is a cycle, a
kind of emotional circuit of
dependence"*

13

F. Guzzardi

Affective dependence is characterized by compulsive obsessiveness and impulsiveness in relating to the other person. There is a clear tendency to put the other first so their wants and needs matter much more than themselves.

The first phase of this cycle is the so-called phase of attraction, in which the emotional dependent, whether man or woman, is attracted by seduction and therefore by the apparent power that someone who is very busy in things, strong, capable of managing their own life, while the emotional dependent feels unable to go it alone and therefore needs someone to make him feel strong and important.

The second phase of the cycle, is called the "phase of the Savior's fantasy", basically a sort of infantile fantasy of the hero who saves the dependent affective is reactivated, feels revitalized by the attention and proximity of the partner, as under the effect of drugs, the partner is idealized and his real characteristics are not clearly seen.

In the third stage, we have relief, the emotional dependent, feels filled, feels important and no longer experiences the feeling of emptiness, hence loneliness and feels valued. This is the so-called phase of the godless.

At this point, **the fourth phase** starts, the one in which there is an increase in the need of the dependent, together with the denial of the partner. In practice, the dependent begins to perceive a growing need for attention and therefore presence. The partner is perceived as essential and begins to escape, becoming less and less present in the relationship. But the emotional dependent, does not want to see these moles with evidence, continually justifying in part and thinking for example that he/she is very busy at work, or he/she has the right to spend some time with friends.

T hus we come to the fifth phase, that of collapse, of negation. Clearly the emotional dependent, analyzes the distancing behaviors and the distance that the partner maintains is something concrete, therefore he starts looking at reality and realizes that he is not central to his partner, consequently the emotional dependent always tries to control more his partner, in an escalation of disputes. At this point, the emotional addict lives an experience of abandonment, he feels that the partner is leaving him and the ancient wounds light up. After parental abandonment (hence the obsessive control behaviors, aimed at the renegotiation of the relationship) the emotional dependent begins to tell friends about being abandoned, seeking the help of others to partially save his relationship. In short, he does everything to bring the behavior of his partner under control but, he does so in abusive ways that are dysfunctional and self-destructive.

W e thus arrive at the sixth phase, that of the withdrawal. The emotional dependent finally realizes that he has been left for someone or something that is more important than him. At this stage, the ancient emotions of emptiness and abandonment, fear, jealousy are reactivated, and at this point in the cycle, the emotional dependent experiences an emotional overload that he cannot manage, the technical name of this situation is "dysregulation. Murderous or suicidal ideas may appear, depression, anxiety, panic and above all obsessive and derivative ideas may appear. At this point, how do you get out of this and learn to have balanced relationships? Obviously, it is necessary to work on some fundamental points, in the meantime start by treating any dependence beyond the emotional dependence, outside the relationship, such as that of food, shopping, alcohol and gaming. It is necessary to recognize addiction, its effects and then work on the ancient painful feelings, linked to the experiences of abandonment and abuse suffered, in order to develop a healthy ability to recognize and assert one's real needs.
In any case, it is advisable to avoid engaging in a romantic relationship until a good level of recovery

from emotional dependence and its underlying mechanisms has been achieved. We keep in mind that there are also the so-called "Romantics chronic" who do not love others but are in love with the idea of love itself, romantic love, these people feed on illusions and live in perpetual expectation of him or the one who will make their dreams come true. We could define these people as romance dependent, so without them, their life becomes trivial, if there are no great emotions or great dramas. So they are people who are inclined to create small tragedies, they cause family quarrels to experience sensations, they can cause damage both to themselves and to others, they play heroin or hero to feel important and powerful. Some of these women find the unripe man arousing, new to them, unpredictable, romantic, the immature man is a charming man. The lunatic would be mysterious and then he could say that the choleric man needs their understanding. Another typical phrase is that: "unhappy man needs our comfort," the inadequate man needs our encouragement and the cold man needs our warmth.

P eople of this kind, have grown up in families where was normally not paid attention to their needs, often there was a subtle violence or hostility between the parents. These People up to the time they were kids, have learned to take refuge in fantasy, or even create special situations but at the base of everything, abandonment is always a trauma that causes suffering. In these relationships, suffering appears oversized, excessive, despair, it is total and takes on the character of a profound, inexplicable despair, without alternatives, without exits. Love is offered with the hope that the other can protect us from fear and instead, fears are acquired with the hope of being reciprocated with ours.

How to get out of this mechanism? Learning to recognize one's own merits, therefore knowing and valuing oneself. This is what I managed to do on myself, after years of suffering, I managed to love myself moderately but sincerely.

"When two people talk to each other"

F. Guzzardi

Personally, I think that love is a symbolic dimension, because it always refers to something else, it refers to something that escapes another meaning behind the manifest one. Therefore loving a person cannot be a quiet thing, as it places the one who loves in a condition of continuous tension and also in a condition of dependence. The one he loves is in a state of amazement, of wonder, in fact love continually surprises us, upsets us, relegating us to a rather passive role and as Freud says: love is characterized as tenacious and irreducible.

A characteristic of this particular feeling is the archaicity of the levels of mental functioning, this means that in the love relationship, the object is idealized and the atmosphere that surrounds it is pregnant with absolute and totalizing sensations that in some sense have the function of protecting us from the ghosts of abandonment. Love is an almost psychotic situation, that is, a condition of fusion with the object that is surrounded by an atmosphere of grandeur. We are captured by this dimension, there is a cancellation of one's own color as regression leads the subject to live a state of deprivation, the ego feels poor and consequently the other becomes a source of life, therefore the possession of this magical object that the other represents is experienced by the ego as a matter of life or death.

But it is also true that the object of love is an object that is impossible to possess, as it is an object of another, that is, of the father or the mother. Now, when two people talk, they interpenetrate, they influence each other and when seduction is triggered, the charm of this phase can become a compulsive and maniacal charm, aimed at compensating for the inferiority of those who are seduced.

Therefore we see that the seduced becomes a greedy person, suffers from the fear of loss, the seduced is addicted, is afraid of abandonment and therefore, a good relationship has the task of reclaiming the quality of desperate love of a pathological emotional dependence. that love tends to unleash. The purpose of a good relationship is to give birth to a healthier feeling, made up of confidence, intimacy and above all a sense of openness, that is, of warmth and mutual trust, which create a relationship based on sincere contact.

Now, this sincere contact is above all of a symbolic nature, that is, it exists as a psychic reality not only as a concrete reality, the symbolic nature of a relationship requires that there be truth, as happens in dreams but does not require that it be something real at all.

The choice of dialogue, of confrontation, therefore, the choice of the relationship which is initially a relationship between the self and the unconscious and subsequently becomes a relationship between the self and the other, this is a transformative choice that leads to action, in the end it is still an action that changes things when we question ourselves, everything begins to change, because thanks to emotional involvement we are pervaded by new forces, old habits disappear and we no longer see reality in simplistic terms such as good or bad or a reality in black and white but we see it symbolically, so we discover the clichés and the falsehoods that we have told ourselves, we see the betrayals towards ourselves and then we want to take the reins of our destiny in hand through a deed of redemption.

14

Love Words

People who often say, "I do this, I do that," are people who have never been loved, no one really cared about them and they don't even know exactly what they want

14

A t the origin of every individuality therefore, there is an imperative of redemption, ignoring this task means remaining entangled in a need for dependence, whoever respects a false desire since it is the desire of only a part of the ego, must then act symbolically, the partial death of the ego has in itself an enormous thirst for life, a thirst for life, behind this death of the ego there is a visceral love for existence; Schopenhauer argued that the suicide loves life but we are talking about symbolic suicide that is not real, the tension towards the symbolic suicide of the ego reveals its transformative values, showing a desire for new life and spiritual rebirth. Jung said that the material man must transform himself into a spiritual man, that is, the man capable of assuming the responsibility of creating himself, here is the ransom, when two people talk to each other all this can happen.

While we talk to another, it is often not the comparison with the other that we seek but we try to realize ourselves through the other. So the other becomes only an instrument in our hands, but in this case, the words that two lovers exchange cannot be words of love. The true love relationship is not based on the word "I'm," but on the instability and lightness, not on the stability and rigidity of the ego.

In affairs of love, construction and destruction take place together, in the true affective relationship the partial crumbling of the boundaries of the ego takes place, in the true relationship of love there is simultaneously exaltation and destructuring of the ego and therefore there is wealth and desolation.

Love is an opening to the symbolic that alludes to something else, which opens to another idyll. Love expresses a psychic reality that is beyond the factual and rational reality of the ego, therefore, love challenges every mechanism and every technique, to cross over into the unclassifiable, saving the individual from conventions, fashions and so on.

Because the relationship is a crossing that leads to a new vision of oneself, and here the will matters little. Instead, letting go, letting oneself be possessed, believing the self in the mystery, what matters is abandoning oneself to the self, the charm and beauty, therefore the symbolic, count a lot.

When the ego in its dominant role steps aside, then the relationship with the other can happen and the ego becomes something different from what it was before the relationship, revealing a part of itself that it never imagined it was. Here the ego changes and stops embodying the exasperated cult of its own subjectivity, "I am this, I am that", entering into a relationship, the ego stops celebrating itself and becomes lateral to make room and welcome the stranger that the other.
The true relationship wants a breaking of the narcissistic shell and therefore, the exposure of its contents which were previously protected and closed in the shell and which are now offered to a stranger.

F. Guzzardi

Intimacy opens up and speaks, shows itself, interacts, lets itself be influenced and contaminated. What was previously intimate becomes shared.
In the relationship the person puts his own loneliness into play and offers it to another, with all the risks that follow from exposing his wounds. Traumas, which were previously closed in the narcissistic shell, are now shared through words. When the words begin to tell these traumas, they drag the subject beyond his own identity and at the same time the subject allows himself to this drag giving the other the possibility to free him from the text of the trauma. This is very similar to the psychotherapy of love that Freud wanted, the suffering subject does not know what to do with the trauma and thanks to an emotional relationship, the trauma becomes an open door to the inner planet, therefore the trauma becomes precious, since it is a wound that it opens the symbolic and shows what lies beyond the real.

Love is also an opening to the symbolic, so it can heal any wound and can take care of everything.

However, in order for the wound to become a center of new energy, the ego must surrender itself to an affective process that it cannot control and cannot even manage. It is said that love is a subversive process in that the order of the ego is perceived, it upsets the stability and identity of the ego because it upsets it, clears it of customs, expropriates it from its property by expanding its borders. This generates fear, but the ego must overcome this fear caused by the undifferentiated, the fear of being shipwrecked but, only if we are willing to be shipwrecked, will we discover new lands.

A love that pull out your hair

Basically, love is when two people talk to each other and a relationship is created. The purpose of a good relationship is to create a sense of openness, therefore of a symbolic nature. This experience allows the being to reach a deep knowledge of himself and of his own psychic mechanisms. This results in a change in 'attitude that leads to' action. The development of the personality therefore means an act of assuming our responsibility in creating a relationship with the other, after all what is necrosis if not an inadequate response to a very important task, that of going beyond ourselves, overcoming those we believe we are, in view of a new person, richer and more creative.

Paraphrasing a song by the Italian singer-songwriter, Fabrizio De Andre`. "Canzone dell'amor perduto" (Song of the lost love).

I would like to talk for the first time about the joys of love, rather than its tragedies, but unfortunately the experience convinced me that happiness does not belong to love, except as its fleeting expression and tenaciously opposed by reality.

If it were not so, probably, being in love would go unnoticed in our consciences like most of the events of daily routine. Because it will seem paradoxical but, man is given to truly enjoy only what has been long awaited.

I suppose that everyone aspires to tranquility and the quiet living of a successful love, of those without too many problems and without great storms, firmly anchored to an unshakable trust in mutual fidelity and so on. The fact is that to conquer such a situation we are also willing to fight, sometimes becoming violent and angry if not completely insane.

To love means, be irremediably compromised, once love becomes part of our life, we only wish that no one would think of upsetting us.

Unfortunately, however, legend has it that love arouses the envy of the gods and not just the gods. Suddenly secret admirers emerge, the betrayed and laconic abandoned.The neighbor hates us because he sees in us the image of fidelity, the one that he has never touched and we know that the neighbour's grass is always better than ours, even our sister would like to change her husband, our mother does nothing but remind us how different it was in her time when love could not be chosen, not to mention what we then put on our own because although satisfied with luck, we would like to make it even more showy we expect from ourselves and from the people we care about, always excellent results, sometimes disproportionate to our and their strengths.

The children must be evident and educated, they must achieve excellent results in school, we must like our work, it must make us earn a lot of money, in short, we fight for a type of existence comparable to that depicted in television commercials where when a group appears familiar it seems that happiness is close at hand.

Certainly we are not the only ones to wake up every day gripped by problems rather than comforted by the joy and enthusiasm of our loved ones and it is understandable that we would like our affairs to go

F. Guzzardi

in quite another way but it does not seem that human existence is structured according to what it is, it is only a desire that is difficult to achieve.

F reud said that life is too hard to be taken as it is, so we need to think about it continually elsewhere and this is a common feature both to madness and to love. Imagine this daydream that collides with everyday life, that is, with those little annoying problems that are nothing in the face of the eternal happiness but which in fact deprive us of its comfort or in any case of its continuity. Even when we are well and feel full of joy and ready to conquer the whole world, we cannot help but wonder about the duration of this condition of well-being and how long we will be able to benefit from this idyll, as if love and its joys should be deserved and only the suffering that precedes them follows them, makes them so. To be loved means to be thought of and the awareness of this makes us invincible, protected by an unassailable armor with which to face the world head on, and this is precisely the source of happiness, a real source devoid of utopian idealizations and above all to the reach of all.

Encountering true love is not a certainty, there are people who spend their entire existence without knowing the meaning of the authentic feeling, this is because the possibility of coming across love always comes from our state of mind, or rather from internal predisposition. At a certain point in life, something can trigger that makes us attentive and selective with respect to the many messages coming from others, our mood and our psychological condition are such as to make us blind and deaf and therefore unable to pick up the signals sent by those who feel attracted to us. The internal disposition enjoys a power, an enormous privilege, is able to make us meet love, to recognize it, to live it, or on the contrary, able to let that train so important pass without stopping in our life.

It is evident that when one is not predisposed from an emotional and psychological point of view, it is almost impossible for an encounter to turn into love, perhaps it will give rise to a temporary relationship, vice versa what happens when being receptive the feeling crosses the gaze of a person who manages to strike us from the first moment, is something mysterious and wonderful, something that we should all experience at least once in our life, the authentic encounter with each other from the genus, I begin a pleasant phase of confusion in which the boundaries between the self and the other no longer exist but there is only an enveloping atmosphere of fusion. For this reason, lovers lose themselves in each other's gaze and their bodies as well as their souls generate a new and fertile unity.

Love, the real one, the one that "tears your hair" and gives that precious desire that allows us to feel young and vital even when the passage of time would like to prevent it, is made above all of silence, is made of long, intense gazes, rich in meanings, which words would never be able to communicate. Being captured by the love dimension makes you become unsuitable to describe it, lovers know well what they feel, they are aware of being immersed in a magma of incandescent emotions, difficult to manage, however, despite this, bringing to light what they are experiencing, it can for them be very difficult, because when you are emotionally involved in a situation and you live it firsthand, you may find yourself lacking the most suitable interpretative tools to deal with it.

Love, like pain, not only invests the soul, it not only has a psychic existence but is written above all in our body which cannot and does not know how to lie. The price to pay is the time to renew and to reimagine oneself, to give voice to one's own intimate nature, to that unexpressed talent that dwells within us, and this work is long and tiring but, this is not enough to make us give up on discovery of ourselves.

The soul in love

S ometimes, I know, it is not easy but, the signs of the body tell you that it is time to change, to leave the bad habit that is so comfortable and easy to repeat every day. So, make it not easy, make it different, make the soul fall in love.

The Greek Soul

I do not mean the soul of the mystics but that of the ancient Greeks, where soul was conceived as your self, your breath or simply your personality. So what is not a body but its lifeblood. The personality therefore falls in love but to live a relationship of equal rank, where neither of the two personalities tries to dominate the other, we need to grow and sip our soul.

Only the soul can fall in love

Only a strong soul will be able to let go of the spell of love which is fugitive, passionate, made up of moments. But in order not to burn everything in the short term of a passion that will leave only a persistent void, we need to manage it with our soul! However, it happens that many people do not have a soul because perhaps in early childhood they were forced to repudiate it, considering it useless for their own growth. So over time they will learn to live without a soul, on the contrary they will get so used to their way of life that they will not even understand what a soul is used for, because they will never know that only the soul can fall in love, the body never fall in love, for anything. We certainly don't need doctrines, religions or anything else that teaches us to love, because this is part of us. Doctor Helen Fisher claims to have studied the brain Brown 75 people over 75 people who were madly in love into a brain scan 17/15 and 17 who are in love long-term people in their 50s.

W ho reported that there were still in love not just loving but in love with their partner long term. You know, we believe that you can't sustain feelings of intense romantic love, well we certainly approve that not right, that's not correct, you can do it, you gotta pick the right person.

The right person

W ell, now we need to understand who the right person is.

Man is, by nature (like all animals without exception), a natural lover, in the sense that this need to love and be loved is imbued within each of us. Of course, apart the cases of personality pathology where there can be an impossibility to love or be loved, as in the pathological narcissism cases for example.

So, we certainly don't need doctrines, religions or anything else that teaches us to love, because this is part of us. Recognizing the right person is also a baggage made of experiences that we carry within us. The right person is the one who responds to our emotional needs but in cases of personality disorders, such as serious emotional shortcomings in the postnatal periods, there is the risk of manipulating, or being manipulated by the chosen partner. In cases of emotional needs never nourished, we will need to fill our inner void without giving anything in return, because we are not used to giving or because our ego has long decided that the love that has been denied us as children, it must be returned to us now with interest and for free, that is, without any emotional exchange on our part. This is the case of pathological narcissists, who created a world where they are and only them at the center of the world while the others are only objects to be used as nourishment to fill an endless inner void.

Empathic animal

In cases of normalcy (but does it really exist?) Where there are no post-natal affective deficiencies, the human being is an empathic animal, that is, that recognizes the pains and emotions of others and allows one to recognize one's own.

Opening up to others is also a sense of self surrender, opening up precisely. This in cases of intimate relationships, leads to the sexual act, which can not be conceived otherwise than as a sense of arrea, to say goodbye to the other, to appear naked, to break down defenses, love is precisely to give oneself but. for this alchemy to work (For a more or less short period) the other must implement the same strategy of surrender, surrender to the other, which is not an act of defeat, or cowardice, to surrender in this chance means handing in, trusting and merging (even if only for a few moments) to become one.

Nature has endowed us with this but also with other terrible things, so let's try to screw nature, using only what we enjoy in our brief passage in this world.

15

A narcissist thing

Living with a pathologically narcissistic person in your life is very painful, far from just being benignly in love with themselves

15

As they are sometimes described, the true pathologically narcissistic person, can be a brutal sadistic manipulator an abuser they're not only not in love with themselves for all intents and purposes they generally cannot love anybody, and this includes you. They will destroy yourself esteem your reputation your family your support system your dreams your life and your very sanity if you allow it and for what seems like no other reason.

You represent everything that they are not, and can never be, they will take it all away from you if you let them. The best advice is to simply stay far away from narcissists once they have been identified in your life, don't talk to them and don't feed into their manipulations you can't help them, they cannot be saved they can only pull you under with them and many of them would truly love to do that. IF the narcissist in your life cannot be avoided here are five things to remember in order to protect yourself:

The narcissist will always use you. Narcissistic People are users they are manipulators they generally don't see other people as living breathing human beings with feelings people are often viewed as either steppingstone to get. What they want to be jumped over on the way to what they want and that's it no matter what they may tell other people no matter what they say this is the truth if we strip away their manipulative words and look only at their actions we actually see this very clearly is who they are and it's more than likely never going to change to put.

It very simply the part of their brain that enables them to care and empathize with other people is either essentially missing or so dysfunctional that is completely ineffective depending on the childhood trauma or other factors. That make them a narcissist in the first place why do narcissists use people?

In a narcissists view, people as objects, extensions of themselves, because of that they are unable to see people as separate beings from themselves with their own feelings, needs, wants and opinions.

"We use our coffee pot, we use our arm, these are objects that serve a purpose in our life and that's all they are we don't worry about whether or not our arm wants to lift a gallon of milk we don't think about if our coffee pot likes making coffee for us, we just make them do, it this is how the pathologically narcissistic person sees and reacts to other human beings a lot of the time. Other people have things they want and they want to absorb these qualities into themselves somehow to make up for what they're lacking they will continue to use you for as long as they think you have something, they want and as long as you will allow it.

F. Guzzardi

Many of them also enjoy manipulating others and they get excitement and pleasure from tricking or getting over on other people it makes them feel smart, powerful and superior.

This is something that more than likely cannot be changed and it's very important that everyone dealing with a narcissist understand this, it's very tempting to view them as helpless when did children who need healing especially the ones who present themselves this way, but narcissists are not children pathologically, narcissistic people cannot be forced to see other people as human beings, is a waste of time, many of them are incapable of doing so and others have no interest.

The narcissist generally in terms of their own psyche, their personality, they don't care how you feel, they have an inability to feel what you feel and so, for this post I want to talk about the narcissist secret weapon and the narcos in the narcissist secret weapon. Remember, narcissists are different levels of narcissism and so, the worst are antisocial personality disorder people who have, their sociopaths and psychopaths and then we have narcissist that we bump into in the grocery store, every day and and so it's important to understand that no narcissist has to be exactly like another narcissist and so, you go back today as you think about people in your life and you know better your family members and spouses or X lovers or whatever you'll be able to understand.

That perhaps, the one quality that they all had, was a lack of empathy or the way they communicated. The degree to their narcissism and to the degree that they were able to be cruel may have differed and so, I believe that the number one tool that narcissists use, is what I call crazy communication like you can't get from point **A** to point **B** with a narcissist, and that's their agenda! So, **A** narcissist is the real codependent because a narcissist absolutely needs a narcissistic supply!

A narcissist need the "body under the bet" and when they feeling a lack of energy, they need someone to control and manipulate, they need someone to be in front of they need, someone that they can actually suck the lifeout, and that will build up their energy.

Crazy communication

Is a sort of sounds like this, and those of you who have experienced it will be able to relate, so in my life the way it showed: "What time you coming home?' That's it a no brainer conversation, an appropriate response would be 5:00 o'clock and then the appropriate behavior would be my husband/wife will come home at 5:00 to 5:00 or 5 after five but generally he'd be home around 5:00 o'clock and life would go on it would be seamless. But when you're dealing with someone who is passive aggressive, are you dealing some went with someone who is a narcissist and they really don't care how you feel and their agenda is to stay above you and never actually equalize with you, it sounds like this: "So babe what time you gonna be home? I'll be home later about what time will you be home so I can start cooking dinner!

"I don't know what time do I usually come home, that's what time I will be on!"

Then they slam the door and you're left standing there like which is happened.

Now if he/she usually comes home around 5:00 o'clock, tonight might come home at 9:00 o'clock and then when you ask him/her what's up e would say something like: "well... I never told you I wasn't going to come home at 9:00 o'clock, what are you so upset about? it's crazy making! or well, you know I knew that you don't like to be disturbed after 6:00 o'clock so that's why I didn't call you!" Like he's the hero or she's the hero or "well I knew that if I called you were going to be fake off... and so you know if you didn't act so crazy when I was going to be late I probably would've called you!"

F. Guzzardi

This is the way they function in the world, it is never *"I'm sorry I didn't give you a clear answer"*. Remember a narcissist's agenda is to create crazy making conversation it's sort of like shadowboxing 3 ghosts; so imagine you're in a boxing ring and you know your shot, you didn't punch in the face from three different boxers, you know with four different boxers and their ghosts you can't see them. So a narcissist's agenda is to keep you off balance and so if you're in a relationship with someone who cannot answer your questions or who fails to give you clear concise answers that's a problem dear one and you will know that by how you feeling. So what I want to do? I want to explain you some ways in which you can learn to protect yourself in a practical sense, because there's a whole lot of talk about what a narcissist is and like I say all the time, we need tools, we need to know what to do when we discover that we're dealing with a narcissist! I see everything in terms of energy and so a narcissist's agenda is to sort of like. They're like vampires, they want to suck the energy out of you and the more depleted you are the better they feel and so and now serves them in a number of ways. If you're dealing with an arm if your husbands a narcissist and he's able to use crazy communication with you or your wife is a narcissist and she's able to make you feel responsible for why she is uncaring for your, feelings then what happens is she gets to witness and he gets to witness your energy drop. Now what happens in the psyche of a narcissist at least I think so, is that helps him feel better than you, they see themselves as more powerful stronger, more in control than you, because you are being drained and losing your fucking live like you're going crazy. A narcissist exploits the needs of a codependent and a narcissist has the ability to make a very nice Co-dependent act extremely irrational.

16

The Hugh

The gesture of the hug gives the feeling of an eternal union, the first experience we try when we come into the world is precisely that of the hug

16

The gesture of the hug gives the feeling of an eternal union, the first experience we try when we come into the world is precisely that of the hug, the child is welcomed in the arms of someone eager to love and care for him, so he feels to be safe, his crying subsides and he falls asleep peacefully.

Being hugged means receiving on a psychological level everything we need to live: love, nourishment, warmth and protection. The hug is essential for the survival of the child but it is also essential for that of the adult. People who never receive hugs or who have received few in childhood are unmistakable, it is possible to recognize them among 1000 because of that hard shell they had to build around their soul. When we are not held in the arms of those we love, we experience an atrocious loneliness where the only possible solution is to strengthen our character to be able to do it alone.

This seems to be the tragic fate of the narcissist, who has a somewhat naive thought, is convinced that he does not need anyone to lean on in order to move forward, believes he is a power, his armor envelops him, his is a hard and refractory narcissistic shell, which hinders any kind of affective contact or emotional participation with the other.

The victim of the narcissist, at some point, perceives that his partner does not want to be hugged as he is not available, because he is wrapped in a sort of barbed wire that prevents access to his soul. Thus, the narcissist risks becoming more isolated, depriving himself of the best aspects of existence and emotions.

The hug is therefore regenerating when it offers the illusion of being able to realize the dream of total Union, in fact, in the arms of the beloved, we finally feel happy as if nothing was missing anymore, as if we had obtained what we have always wanted. , the hug is a powerful means of communication, through this gesture, we can communicate to the person we love those emotions that we would not have been able to express through words alone and at the same time, when we are hugged, we hear the words of the other, which are words full of meanings, which in that silent instant describe inexpressible feelings of satisfaction.

The hug can express the intensity of a feeling or the depth of an emotion, so it is a difficult experience for the narcissist, who is more used to using words rather than physical contact, with words the narcissist can easily lie while when we find ourselves tight in the arms of the other person it is no longer possible to lie, our truth emerges with arrogance, waiting for a reaction from the other. The narcissist's embrace is mechanical, a bit false, rather muscular, like his sexuality on the other hand, his embrace is tragic, as it leaves a sense of despair, paradoxically appears grotesque and caricatured, if it were a prelude to separation.

We could define it in a certain sense, a poignant embrace but devoid of emotion, there is a lot of technique in the narcissist's embrace, the movement is studied, calculated, is adjusted to create the maximum effect but it is an embrace that is empty, dull , lifeless, it does not communicate love.

The narcissist is a person who loves to look at himself and is pleased with his physical appearance, he feels satisfied by the admiration of others and therefore is a vain type, the vain bets everything on the outward appearance, the vain act moved by a single need, that of being admired and desired by others, therefore, they are unwilling to give, they prefer to draw attention to them. The narcissist has a morbid love for his own image, focuses all his interest, all his energy on himself, is obsessed with appearing and this on a psychological level and a sterile withdrawal on himself, having himself as unique landmark.

Who loves his own image, leaves no room for others

and has nothing to offer to the people around him, in practice, the narcissist transforms the philosophy of appearing into a faith and is in love with his own image, so he believes he is the center of the universe and forgets that others exist around him but his belief that he can be happy only because he is admired for his physical appearance is an unreal illusion, therefore the narcissist is self-centered and cannot be available for relationships with others, he has no interest or energy to devote to anyone who is exiled from his small world but beware, this is not a conscious behavior but a dynamic that takes note independently of the will, it is a need that arises from fragility, he must protect himself from involvement affective, because it could shatter his easy self, therefore he raises barricades around him, which prevent others from accessing his inner world, here is because the narcissist's embrace is fake. The narcissist is alone and is enveloped in his emptiness.

J ung says: *"Destroy the memory that you are, forget who you were and what you wanted"*. There are people who have neither the courage nor the inner drive to live the overcoming of the past and the insecurity that derives from it, the lack of reference points, which means destroying all the securities that allow you to live in a reassuring way but, to live in uncertainty it is a task of maturity so what?

Strong are those people who never stop questioning themselves, who never retreat from the risk and accept the greatest of all challenges, that of unconditional adherence to their own inner values from which life is born as a form of redemption. In this vision, the obstacle exists as an incentive to move forward not to stop, the resolution of our most intimate problems always passes through the conquest of awareness and therefore of the capacity for action and through the desire for change, which essentially means, be aware of the importance of others and therefore of the humanity present around us."

Do we really have freedom?

F. Guzzardi

In this perspective, man is a being in the world whose existence represents the very condition of knowledge. Men inhabit the world, they are in the world and psychopathology is also a being in the world, that is, a way in which the individual inhabits the world. This is the basic principle from which existential dialysis moves, which for no reason wants to isolate psychopathological phenomena from the global context in which these phenomena are inserted, therefore human freedom is not unlimited but is conditioned by a sort of existential to priori, that is, that foundation in which individuals find themselves thrown. The world project is another way of defining the response that an individual is providing to the foundation of his existence. The world project becomes the sphere that will condition all the behavior of a person and therefore, the choices. In personality disorders, something of the individual has crystallized, the world project has crystallized, which has become limited and adequate. , continuously opposes a halt to the realization of the individual's potential. The project of the world becomes the system of the modes of existence of an individual and the latter are also expressed in the field of interpersonal relationships.

Therefore authenticity and alienation, the possibility of making choices and the more these choices conform to the foundation of an existence, the more they are rich in creative and satisfying potential. Respecting one's authenticity is the only way to be beyond the world, that is, to somehow overcome the anguish of being thrown into the world. When the lifestyle of a human being is predominantly authentic, his opinions, goals and choices are characterized by precision and originality, whereas those of an inauthentic individual tend to be vague and stereotyped. The former is active and influential while the latter is passive in relating. In interpersonal relationships, the authentic person aims at the dual mode, that is, at intimacy while the inauthentic person gets lost in the formal and superficial relationships that are typical of the plural mode. Authenticity generally coincides with the ability to change, to evolve, to mature, to change attitudes, whereas in the inauthenticity, instead, the tired, the paralysis from which it is difficult to return, human hope of failure, that is of the frustration of the limit, correspond it is tolerated by being inauthentic and in the face of this experience falls into psychopathology.

One must have chaos within oneself to generate a dancing star.

To conclude, we can say that vitality, strength, the possibility of inner youth are directly proportional to the recharging attitude. The individual is characterized by his own potential and therefore, we must show the courage to respond to the call of our existence, regardless of the obstacles that each one will encounter, must have the courage to give an answer to his being in the world and the goal is not important. that at the end of life we will have reached but, what really matters, is our path.

17

Just let it happen and it happens

When someone comes to you to tell you about a wound, a wound that still tears him now, after so many years; invite him to seek the darkness within himself, the inner emptiness.

F. Guzzardi

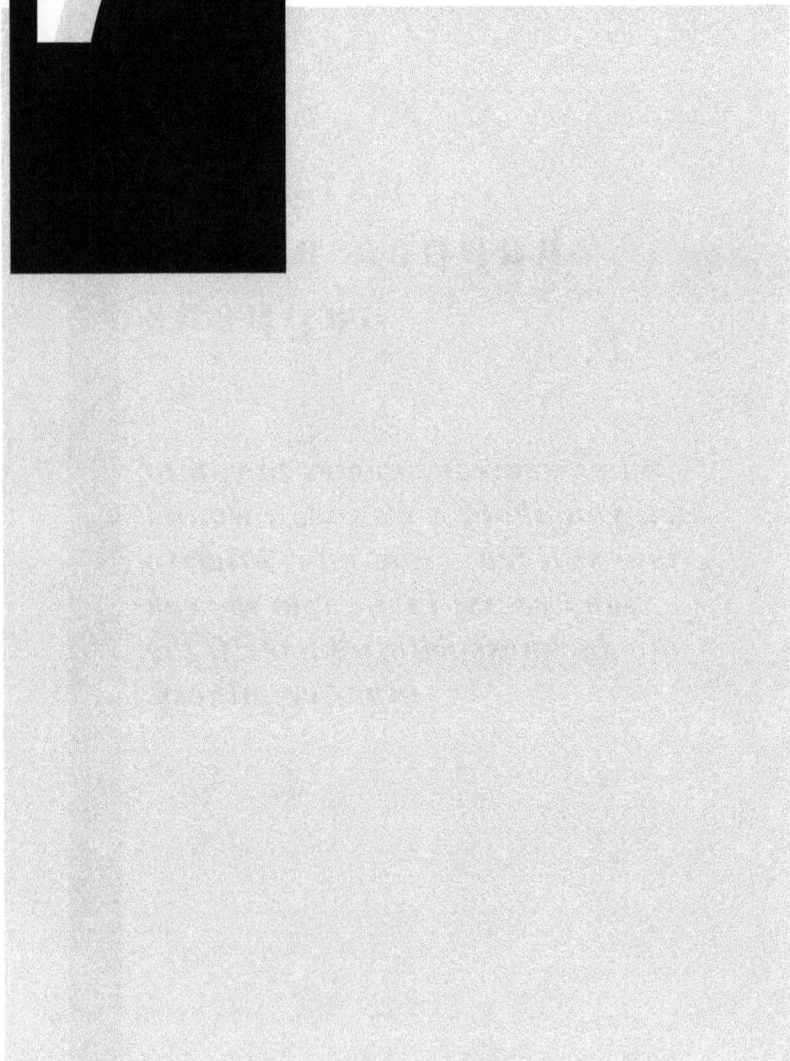

I n short, oblivion has immense power over the soul and even more has its distraction, that is, the ability to detach oneself from the traumas of the past. There is a territory within us, where we exist without the wound and that territory is the Kingdom of images where time no longer exists and things become infinite.

Eyes closed, they are able to see images, wonderful images. Activate the ancient circuits of the brain, because dreaming is the foundation of being, another territory of consciousness in which images live and the place that has the right energy to make us discover that we are not only the children of our parents; the soul has its strength elsewhere, far from the facts to which we attribute importance which they do not have, an importance which is not true for the psychic world. I think that oblivion, mystery, are cures while the obsession with explaining, the obsession with understanding, with thinking about traumas, is the disease of this century.

Healing takes place only if you go out of the ego, if you go out of memories. Memories of common thought, memories linked to reasoning. Even if the suffering has been going on for a long time, it can end in an instant if we change the way we look at ourselves.

Dreams that have never come true can be realized out of the blue, just change the way you look at them. What the willpower has not been able to produce, the distraction has magically achieved. The brain is capable in every instant of producing substances that heal wounds, it is a question of letting the kingdom of the night take over, it is a question of yielding, it is a question of not continuing to think about it; every time your wound comes to mind, immediately look for the image that removes the trauma: a flying eagle, a princess in a castle, an egg that hatches, a Sylvester landscape, a flower, a tree . The images They are the Kingdom of energies, just call them to enter the territory of care; whenever the thought of trauma comes, you imagine, the rest comes by itself. The images open the circuits of the brain that introduce the right substances into the body. We can be happy within all kinds of truths.

F. Guzzardi

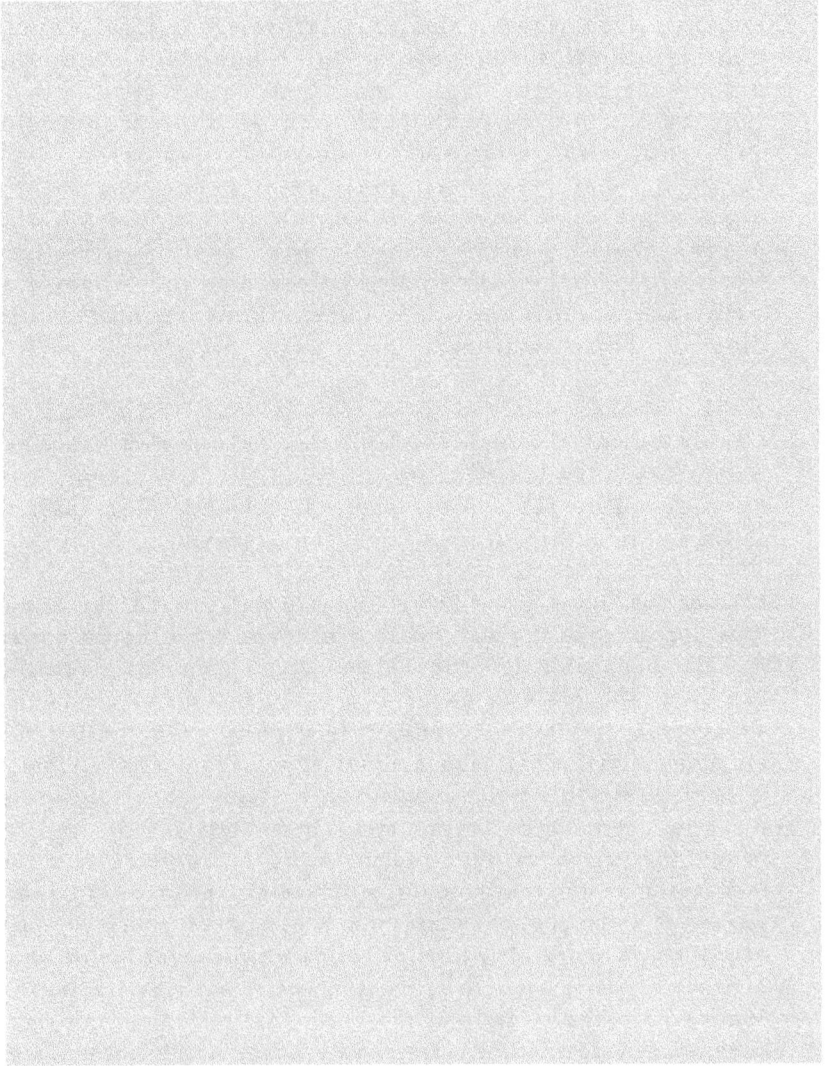

About the author

F.Guzzardi is an Italian-born author who lives and works in Florida, USA. He collaborate with the American magazine, *I'M Italian*. In this book he tells us about a hidden reality of our soul but he does it from the point of view of the victim. The wounds of the soul that affect our entire life.

Other books by the author: Silent Love (L''amore non detto) 2021, Hoffmann & Hoffmann / 26 Giorni (Italian) 2019 Hoffmann & Hoffmann.

F. Guzzardi

The sick Love

F. Guzzardi

www.ingramcontent.com/pod-product-compliance
Lightning Source LLC
Chambersburg PA
CBHW022338280326
41934CB00006B/686